Rodney Legg is best known i
and historian of its offshore i:
Bristol Channel. His current
Steep Holm Legends and History, Steep Holm at War and Steep Holm: Allsop Island, documenting it from mythological and geological times to its current role as a nature reserve memorial to author and broadcaster Kenneth Allsop.

His archaeological credentials include the transcription and annotation, for editor John Fowles, of the first edition of John Aubrey's *Monumenta Britannica*, which had lain unpublished in the Bodleian Library at Oxford for nearly three centuries. He followed this with his own *Romans in Britain* and has documented the *Stonehenge Antiquaries*.

Here Legg turns his attention closer to home, following in Aubrey's footsteps, to show that the remarkable timber and stone circles at Stanton Drew formed a solar and lunar calendar. Its key alignments gave the two vital turning points of the year, pointing to the first sky-glow of Midsummer Day over Hautville's Quoit, and to the Midwinter Solstice as the Sun dropped down behind the Cove beside the Druids' Arms.

STANTON DREW

Great Western Temple

Rodney Legg

Wincanton Press
National School, North Street,
Wincanton, Somerset BA9 9AT

For John Newcombe –
the publican with stones
in his garden

First published 1998
Copyright © 1998
Permission is hereby given for extracts to be quoted by
anyone researching the enigma of Stanton Drew,
provided that the source is duly acknowledged.
International standard book number 0 948699 64 7

Printed in Somerset by FWB Printing
at Bennetts Mead, Wincanton. Typeset there,
in New Baskerville, by Vanessa Spratling.
Distributed by Halsgrove, Lower Moor Way, Tiverton,
Devon EX16 6SS, telephone 01-884-243-242

Contents

Stanton Drew — Location and Walks
SKETCH MAP

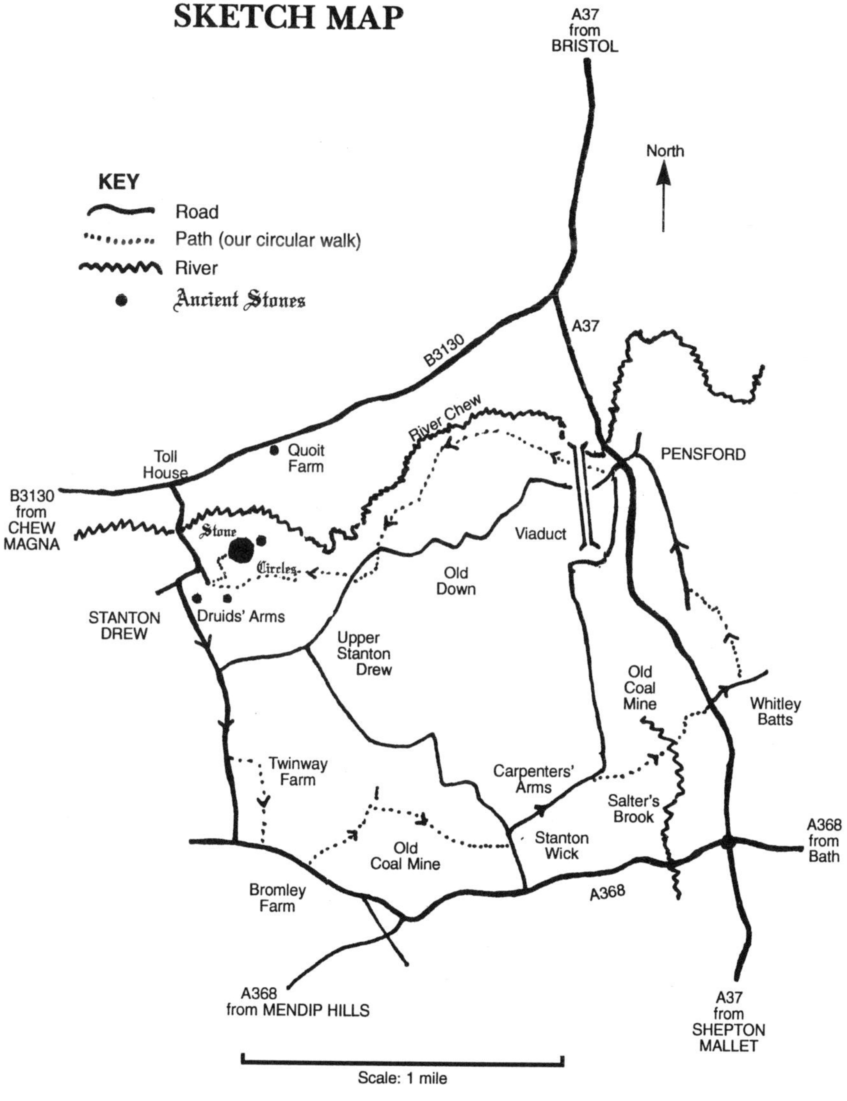

A37
from
BRISTOL

North

KEY

~~ Road
•••••••• Path (our circular walk)
~~~~ River
• Ancient Stones

B3130

A37

River Chew

Toll
House

Quoit
Farm

PENSFORD

B3130
from
CHEW
MAGNA

Stone

Circles

Viaduct

Old
Down

STANTON
DREW

Druids' Arms

Upper
Stanton
Drew

Old
Coal
Mine

Whitley
Batts

Twinway
Farm

Carpenters'
Arms

Salter's
Brook

A368
from
Bath

Old
Coal Mine

Stanton
Wick

Bromley
Farm

A368

A368
from MENDIP HILLS

A37
from
SHEPTON
MALLET

Scale: 1 mile

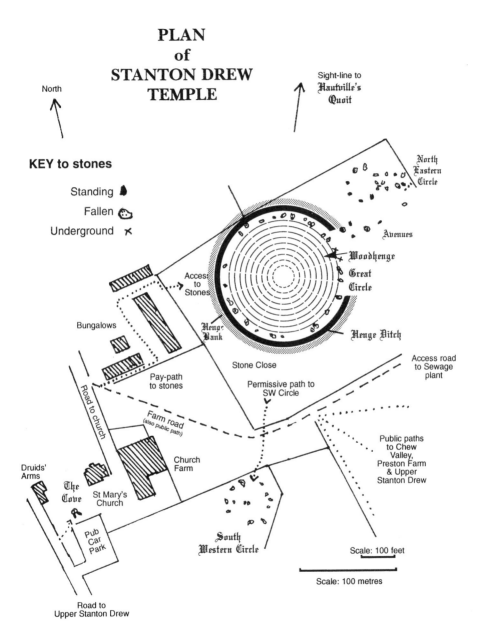

PLAN
of
STANTON DREW
TEMPLE

North

Sight-line to
Hautville's
Quoit

KEY to stones

Standing 🌢
Fallen 🐚
Underground ✗

North Eastern Circle

Avenues

Woodhenge

Great Circle

Access to Stones

Bungalows

Henge Bank

Henge Ditch

Access road to Sewage plant

Stone Close

Pay-path to stones

Permissive path to SW Circle

Road to church

Farm road
(also public path)

Church Farm

Public paths to Chew Valley, Preston Farm & Upper Stanton Drew

Druids' Arms

The Cove

St Mary's Church

Pub Car Park

South Western Circle

Scale: 100 feet

Scale: 100 metres

Road to
Upper Stanton Drew

7

Wood to Stone

Stanton Drew as a monument is the product of continuous evolution for a period of 1,500 years. From 3000 to 2500 BC it existed as a Neolithic earthen henge. Around 2500 BC the interior of this circle was levelled and rebuilt as a complex wooden henge.

Only in the Wessex Culture period of the Bronze Age, from 2100 through to 1500 BC, did the laying out take place of the stone circles which comprise the visible elements of the monument today.

Some aspects of the evolving monument probably co-existed for several centuries but the meadows as we see them are now virtually flattened apart from multiple circles of stones, most of which have fallen. Others are totally covered and have been located by probing.

Centrepiece of the series of monuments, in the meadows on the south side of the River Chew six miles south of Bristol, is the 365-feet diameter Great Circle. The figure is the blatant clue to its purpose as a calendar. Its stones stand inside the former ditch and flattened bank, back-filled into this interior ditch at the end of the Neolithic period, which comprised the original Neolithic henge monument. The overall size of this earthwork was some 450-feet in diameter, with a formidable V-shaped ditch on the inside, 30-feet wide, which must have degenerated into a moat given the proximity of the water table and continuing propensity of these pastures to flood.

That may have hastened the evolution of the site, though its original choice and aspect must have been in the knowledge that these are low-lying wetlands. That, at least, would have given them wide and deep horizons if there was an astronomical imperative to the distant sight-lines, in the same way that the other two premier Wessex circles at Stonehenge and Avebury are positioned in landscapes that are blandly flat. Unlike those chalky uplands, however, what limited rises and skyline knolls that Stanton Drew does offer, those beside the Chew valley are almost entirely lacking in burial mound profiles. Stanton Drew seems to have performed for the religion of the living rather than the dead.

Stage two, inside the great ditch of the henge monument, was a Woodhenge of immense timber poles, many of which were probably carved with curves and spirals as seen cut in stone at the famous Irish chambered tomb of New Grange. As well as these totem poles there may well have been phallic shapes, given the number of chalk-cut phalluses found in the ditch of the Neolithic henge beneath Maumbury Rings Roman amphitheatre at Dorchester, Dorset.

Monuments such as this probably served a dual purpose as ritual centres and gathering places for the tribe as well as a form of cosmic computer, with holes into which posts of varying heights could have been slotted and moved around as necessary, in order to compute the phases of the moon and make other astronomical and calendar projections. The evidence elsewhere for such empty sockets comes from the Aubrey Holes around Stonehenge.

Stanton Drew's Great Circle has nine concentric rings of holes — empty or formerly holding oak pillars — ranging from 300 feet in diameter at the extremity down to 60 feet for the central circle.

They were revealed by a ground level magnetometer

survey carried out for English Heritage archaeometry specialist Andrew David, and released by their chief archaeologist, Geoffrey Wainwright, in November 1997.

The magnetometer sensed the sub-surface disturbance of the post holes without the need for conventional digging. Though it confirmed the presence of the Woodhenge rather than its artistry, Dr Wainwright believes the uprights were decorated, as with contemporary pottery which carries spiral motifs and geometrical patterns:

> It is hard to think of a structure like this with nine concentric circles not being carved in some way. Neolithic patterns are quite stylised and relate to tribal territories, we believe. It would be very surprising if these motifs were not replicated on the timber uprights.

The end for the Woodhenge, filling its surrounding ditch with water and landslipped earth, possibly came in the flash-floods that followed in the climatic chaos triggered by the meteorite bombardment from the direction of Jupiter's orbit which peppered the Earth in about 2350 BC. Their parent asteroids follow the orbit of Jupiter but are periodically disturbed by the gravitational influence of Saturn.

Freak weather consequently caused economic and cultural collapse across the Mediterranean states, with refugees and agricultural anarchy upsetting the status quo northwards through Europe. Quite apart from its disruption of what became disfunctional societies, the sustained rainfall would have done considerable physical damage to the site, floating and rotting its sacred timbers.

The Jupiter meteorite shower, recurrent every 1,500 years, was identified by Dr Benny Peiser, an anthropologist of John Moores University, Liverpool, and astrophysicist Victor Glube of Oxford University. It is next destined to pass Earth in about 2150 AD.

Later encounters with our planet, so far, have lacked the cataclysmic proximity of the 2350 BC shower.

The Trojan asteroids have the same orbit as Jupiter, half behind and half in front of the planet. Both clusters are disturbed by the regular passing of Saturn. Sometimes a large chunk is sent hurtling into the inner solar system.

Midsummer and Midwinter Calendar

Quite apart from whatever complexities can be computed with individual stones of the rebuilt monument, the five Bronze Age Wessex Culture groupings at Stanton Drew are set to delineate the two key solar events of the year.

A line drawn through the middle of both the South Western Circle and the Great Circle and extended north-north-east, an angle of 20 degrees east of north, points to the skyline monolith of Hautville's Quoit which would have been silhouetted at just one crucial time of the year. On 21st June, as we know it, in 2000 BC or thereabouts it would have been touched by the start of the sky-glow before the Sun rises on Midsummer Day. Indeed, the longest day.

That is the northern extremity then closer to north, of what would have appeared to ancient peoples as the Sun's orbit around us; a date for celebrations and a marker for the harvest to come. At its other extreme, the shortest day, the Sun's ultimate constricted appearance — or disappearance, rather — is marked by the alignment of the North Eastern Circle, with a line through its centre, and again the middle of the Great Circle, extending south-west to the Cove on the opposite skyline. That is a point 240 degrees around the compass from map north.

So the Cove marks the Midwinter Day sunset of the shortest day, on 21st December. This again was and is, these days with Christmas, a time of festivities. It is also a key date in the agricultural calendar for calculating dates of ploughing and planting.

Therefore Stanton Drew performs as a solar calendar

to mark the two natural extremes of the year, six months apart. Around it the season turned. The angles of 2100 to 2000 BC have now shifted eastwards at sunrise (further away from north) and westwards at sunset (towards north) due to the wobble of the Earth's spin, or precession and obliquity of the ecliptic as the 26,000-year cycle is variously known. The chances of such alignments occurring simply by random chance are 129,240 to one against.

As for sunrise on Midwinter Day, the Avenues eastward from the Great Circle and south-east from the North Eastern Circle point towards its appearance and could have been linked with further skyline stones that are now missing, on the first wave of hills towards Old Down and Pensford. Not that there are any records of such stones.

Antiquarian Folklore

The first recorded references to the stones at Stanton Drew come in the manuscript of *Monumenta Britannica* by the 17th-century antiquary John Aubrey [1626-97]. He had heard of the monument from his grandfather's widow who married Bristol alderman John Whitson and lived four miles from Stanton Drew, at Burnett Manor.

Aubrey's account, written in 1664, is nothing if not detailed. For this Aubrey would not have apologised. Answering criticism in another context, he realised he might be regarded as too trivial and minute in his attention to detail.

But a hundred years hence that minuteness will be grateful, he replied.

I quoted this when I published the first printed version of his meticulous account of the personified stones of Stanton Drew; not in 1664, that is, but for the eventual production of *Monumenta Britannica* in 1980. At Stanton Drew:

... behind the manor house is this ancient monument which they call the Bride. All the account they can give of it is this tradition, that a bride going to be married, she and the rest of the company were metamorphosed into these stones. One of the stones they call the Bride and another is called the Parson's stone, and another the Cook's stone.

These stones are nine or ten feet high and as hard as marble, and it seems to be of the very same sort with [St] Vincent's Rock near Bristol; about seven miles hence. In some there is iron ore: so likewise in those rocks. They are of several tons. This monument is far bigger than Stonehenge: the diameter is about ninety paces.

I could not perceive any trench about is as at Avebury, Stonehenge &c: It is in ploughed land and so easily worn out.

The "corn was ripe" at the time of Aubrey's visit, so he could not measure the stones as he wished, and he writes that the villagers break them "with sledges, because they so encumber their good land, and they told me they are much diminished within these few years".

Some stones "seem to be the remainder of the Avenue as at Kennet [leading from Avebury] and reach in length about half a quarter of a mile". They might be "leading to another temple as from West Kennet to the monument on the top of the hill" [Overton Hill Sanctuary].

"About a quarter of a mile hence is another great stone called Hakewell's Coyte, which may be what only remains of the like monument. There lived anciently in these parts one Hakewell, a person of power and mighty strength, he lies buried in Chew church where he hath a monument. It is very probable that the village hath its name of Drew from the Druids." 'Drew' has since been said to come from Drogonis, which is Norman French. Stanton Drew means "Drogo's village with the stones". By 1291 this Stanton Drogonis suffix had become Stanton Dru.

Further into the manuscript, Aubrey refers to the stones, collectively, as "The Wedding" and again gives the tradition of the bride and the rest of the company being "metamorphosed into these stones". In case anyone should think he is taking any of this seriously, Aubrey goes on to describe the "encroachment of ignorance on mankind" and the "strange absurdities man can by custom and education be brought to believe".

"Hakewell's Coyte [Hautville's Quoit] "is a stone a good distance off" which Aubrey compared in location with the hilltop Sanctuary at West Kennet and isolated stones in the vicinity of other stone circles such as the Heel Stone at Stonehenge and King's Stone at the Rollrights, in Oxfordshire.

Stanton Drew features in Robert Gay's eclectic manuscript of the 1660s entitled *A Fool's Bolt soon shott at Stonage*. Stonage is Stonehenge; Gay was rector of Nettlecombe on Exmoor; and the tome eventually found publication, anonymously, in Peter Langtoft's Chronicle of 1725:

At Stanton Dru, six miles on the south of Bristol, are eight stones, bigger than the greatest of those at Stonage, but their tops broken off, so that they are not above 12 foot high standing circularly, and round about, within 200 yards of those eight are, at least 60 more smaller stones, 6, 7, or 8 foot high, standing upright. This was an old British Trophie, as may appear by the name thereof, retained still in the name of the parish, in which it stands, viz Stanton Dru, 'the Stone Town of Victory'. Secondly, by the smaller stones, monuments of the conquerors' friends there slain, one of which being lately fallen, in the pit, in which it stood, were found the crumbs of a man's bones, and a round bell, like a large horse-bell, with a screw as the stem of it; whence I conjecture, that as the circle of large stones was the Trophy of Victory, so those smaller were monuments of friends slain in winning the Victory (for Victors would not honour their enemies with such monuments) and the bell was part of an old Briton's weapon, there buried with its owner, and, I suppose the like bones and bells may be found under the other small stones, confirming the premis.

Aubrey's antiquarian successor, William Stukeley [1687-1765], was the next quasi-archaeological visitor, in the company apparently of map-maker Dr John Strachey in July 1723. Stukeley's description is of "The Weddings", now plural:

Several of the stones of the outer circles stand on the other side of the hedge, and two or three are sunk into the ditch: those are vulgarly called the Fiddlers, as the others the Maids, or the revel rout attendant on a marriage festival; for the people of this country have a notion, that upon a time of a couple were married on a Sunday, and the friends and guests were so prophane as to dance upon the green together, and by a divine judgement were thus converted into stones: so I suppose the two stones so close together in the inner circle were reputed the Bride and Bridegroom; the rest were the Company dancing, and the Fiddlers stood on the outside. I have observed this notion and appellation of Weddings, Brides, and the like, is not peculiar to this place, but applied to many other of these Celtic monuments about the kingdom; as the Nine Maids in Cornwall, nine great stones set all in a row: whence possibly one may conjecture, in very ancient times, it was a custom here, even of the Christians, to solemnise marriage and other holy rites in these ancient temples, perhaps before churches were built in little parishes ...

The Georgian architect John Wood [1705-54], in his *Description of Bath*, published in 1749, adds the tradition that these are countless stones:

No one, say the country people about Stantondrue, was ever able to reckon the number of these metamorphosed stones, or to take a draught of them, though several have attempted to do both, and proceeded till they were either struck dead upon the spot, or with such an illness as soon carried them off.

Stanton Drew is in good megalithic company with this tradition, which is shared with Stonehenge and the Rollright Stones, as well as lesser known monuments from Cornwall to Kent.

As for the wedding party, being turned to stone for dancing on a Sunday, an identical tradition attaches to the stones of la Noce de Pierre at Finisterre in Brittany.

Other folklore — or "fakelore" — had yet to evolve, such as in the 1870s when Dr James Fergusson popularised a thesis that "megalithic remains are of more recent date than is generally supposed". His theory developed into a book on *Rude Stone Monuments in all Countries, their Age and Uses*.

The Arthurian legends were back in vogue, being turned into Victorian romantic literature, and Somerset inevitably featured in the stories, since John Selden had written in 1622 that "By South Cadbury is that Camelot". As for Stanton Drew, Fergusson asserted, the stones belonged to the Arthurian age after the collapse of Roman Britain, and commemorated the eleventh battle of King Arthur. This had been fought around Maes Knoll, after battles at Caerleon on Usk and the Severn crossing, but ahead of the twelfth and final victory on Mount Badon, which was identified as one of Bath's seven hills.

The Stones

Countless they may be, according to legend, but William Stukeley gives the total as 160. That was probably an exaggeration; just about half that are visible today, including those that are fallen or barely visible through the grass. Most are hard reddish locally-found conglomerate, which glisten in the rain, though a handful have been said to be oolitic limestone from Dundry, three miles to the north-west.

Hautville's Quoit is the more interesting exception, being a sarsen boulder from the Marlborough Downs, and it is possible one or two other stones were also hauled from there; a massive megalithic undertaking, but quite credible as an achievement of a people capable of moving 40-ton rocks across the Vale of Pewsey and Salisbury Plain to rebuild Stonehenge.

The Great Circle

Leslie Grinsell compiled the pamphlet on the monument for the Ministry of Works, its legal guardians prior to the era of English Heritage, back in 1956. In this guide he gives the diameter of the circle as 365 to 370 feet in a line across it from north-to-south, "and very slightly less east-to-west, being not quite circular" (Ordnance Survey map reference ST 600 633).

Most prehistoric stone circles were slightly elliptical. He notes the rather irregular spacing of the stones. This may imply that some are missing, perhaps being removed for building since Stukeley's count, but 27 is the present total, of which only a couple are standing. The recumbent ones are assumed to have originally stood; indeed Charles Darwin, in his rather esoteric work on the action of earthworms, explains how such stones, in much firmer soil than this at Stonehenge, have been de-established by three millennia of micro-earthmoving.

Stone Close — as the field is known which contains the Great Circle, North Eastern Circle and their Avenues — has been a cow pasture for decades but at the time of John Aubrey's visit, in the summer of 1664, it was arable land, under standing barley.

There may or may not be any significance in the fact that the two noticeable gaps — of 100 feet at the north-west side, and 90 feet in the southern arc of the Great Circle — are similar in width. Grinsell is probably close to the mark when he suggests "there were originally at least 30" stones, if only because that would give the number for a lunar calculator to provide the days of the moon's phases, to complement the solar calendar established by the sight-lines through the centres of the three circles.

The size of the stones varies greatly, though there are larger parts of some, invisible beneath the ground. They are in the region of five to ten feet in length.

John Aubrey's plan: 'The Wedding' at Stanton Drew in the 1660s

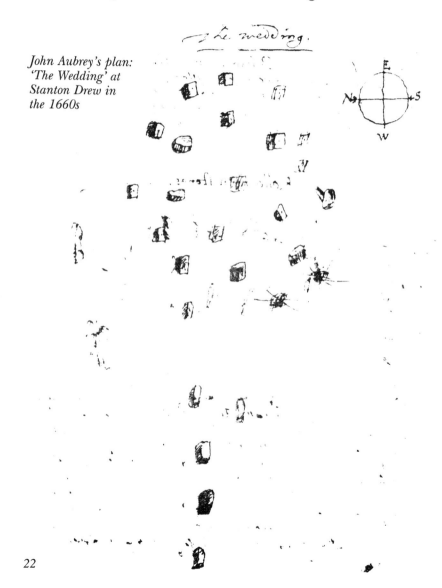

The Avenues

Set southwards of a line drawn between the middle of the North Eastern Circle and the Great Circle, and therefore not obstructing its key mid-summer sight-line to the evening sun disappearing behind The Cove, are the 13 stones of an Avenue about 25 feet wide (ST 601 633).

Of this, probably, there were many more stones in Stukeley's time; indeed there are two alignments with a second avenue turning off the first to approach the North Eastern Circle from a direction approximating to south-south-east.

Some of the surviving stones are big, and five are standing. These are up to eight feet in height. Grinsell writes that these avenues extend "towards the River Chew".

However, it is difficult to see the eastern course of the river, and it is very likely that it was even more treeful in prehistoric times.

Instead, as the focal point, it is tempting to think that there was a skyline stone set on the first wave of hills toward Old Down and Pensford (ST 609 633), in the region of where the lane crosses the hill. This is due east from the Great Circle.

The other avenue, from the North Eastern Circle, is set east-south-east, with the two converging in the hedgerow about 200 feet from the North Eastern Circle and 350 feet from the outer edge of the Great Circle.

The alignment from the North Eastern Circle points towards the higher ground where a public path crosses fields on the south side of the same hill. Here is another place for a stone search (ST 609 631).

They were placed, perhaps, for the sky-glow and sunrise on Midwinter Day, so the monument could determine and celebrate the solstices in their entirety.

John Aubrey's manuscript:
'The Wedding' at Stanton
Drew from Monumenta
Britannica

North Eastern Circle

This is the best preserved segment of the monument, being as Grinsell records, 97 to 100 feet in diameter, and comprising eight huge stones, "all still in excellent condition, the four south-western ones standing" (ST 601 634). He notes, interestingly, that they are "positioned on the principle of opposing pairs of stones equidistant from the centre, as distinct from arrangement on the circumference of a circle previously marked out from the centre with the aid of a cord".

Their layout is complicated at the eastern quadrant by "a group of nine stones not fully explained, but at least three of them are in fact broken parts of one large block, which may have formed the first stone of the Avenue".

Leslie Grinsell comes into his own with these observations, worthy of a latter-day John Aubrey, and as the leviathan of modern archaeological fieldwork, Grinsell shared Aubrey's passion for folklore and gossip. It was my pleasure to find a few of the barrows that he had missed, in Dorset, and to have had his co-operation through Bill Hoade on the project to publish *Monumenta Britannica*.

Grinsell also produced a booklet on the Stanton Drew legends; I feel honoured to follow in his footsteps.

South Western Circle

From the largest stones to the least, down to half size in length and only a fraction when it comes to weight, the South Western Circle has its centre 600 feet west-south-west from the middle of the Great Circle (ST 599 631).

Formerly in the south-east corner of a small orchard — the boundaries of which bent around it — the stones are now in a pasture which stretches northwards to the road beside the car-park of the Druids' Arms.

Eleven stones, all now fallen, are set in a circle with a diameter of 140 to 145 feet. At least one stone is missing. Two smaller stones, close to the centre, apparently mark the viewing point for the observation of the midsummer sunrise at Hautville's Quoit.

Hautville's Quoit

The demise of a once substantial outlying stone, set on an alignment drawn through the centres of the South Western Circle and Great Circle and projected north-eastwards, was caused by its proximity to the main road, on the rise to the east of the exquisite gnome-like thatched turnpike Toll House (ST 602 638). Here it gives its name to Hautville Quoit Farm, though John Aubrey, writing in 1664, calls it Hakewell's Coyte:

> The common people tell this incredible story that Hakewell stood upon the top of Norton Hill, about half a mile off where the Coyte now lies, and coyted it down to this place; for which having the Manor of Norton given him, and thinking it too little, did give it the name of Norton mal-reward, which they pronounce small reward.

The manor of Norton, in the parish of Chew Magna, was granted to Sir John Hautville, by Edward I, for services rendered in the Crusades. Hence the suffix Malreward, because Sir John thought it hardly adequate as the royal thank you for his endurances across the Mediterranean and through Palestine. The derisory name was in use, on legal documents, by 1327.

As for Hautville's Quoit, William Stukeley claims a second stone, close by, and names them "Hautvil's Coyts". Not that Stukeley has the reliability of Aubrey, though the stone could not yet have been split for its roadmaking role as it had grown from 10 feet 6 inches given by Aubrey to 13 feet when visited by Stukeley in 1723. By the time C. W. Dymond came to it, in 1896, it was reduced to its present 7 feet.

John Collinson, compiling Somerset's county history in 1791, quotes the "common proverbial rhyme" of "Stanton Drew, a mile from Pensford, and another from Chew," and goes on to give a delightful vignette of a pastoral landscape on "reddish strong loam, loosened by a little sand. Elm is the principal timber, which flourishes here in great luxuriance." As indeed it did, until the great plague of beetle-borne fungus arrived from Holland and the south in the 1970s.

Collinson gives a detailed description of Hautville's Quoit and the beginning of its abuse for the provision of roadstone:

The River Chew washes this parish, and runs under a stone bridge northward from the church in its way to Pensford. The road to that town from Chew passes to the north of this river, and in the road lies an immense stone called Hautville's Coit (a name it has sustained for many ages) and is by tradition reported to have been thrown hither by that gigantic chamption Sir John Hautville, from Mays Knolle Hill [Maes Knoll], upwards of a mile distance, the place of his abode. The tump on that hill is also affirmed to have been the cleanings of the same man's spade; and so confident are the common people of the reality of the manoeuvre, that a farmhouse erected of late years near the coit, was distinguished by the title of Hautville's Coit Farm, which doubtless it will preserve till records are no more.

This stone was formerly of vast magnitude, being computed to have weighed upwards of thirty tons; but the waggon loads of fragments that have been broken from it at different times, for the purpose of mending the roads, have diminished its consequence as to bulk and appearance, though not as to antiquity or the design of its erection; for it was part of a very remarkable monument of antiquity, which has distinguished this parish for many ages, and has diverted the steps of many a traveller.

Hautville's Quoit lies on the south side of the road, just east of what has now been shortened to Quoit Farm, and has been in a fallen state since the Middle Ages. It would originally have been a standing stone. In geology as well as position it may be different from the other stones of local conglomerate, as it has been claimed as a sarsen boulder from the Wiltshire chalklands.

If this is substantiated, given the immense effort that would have been needed to haul it here, it would have been both a physical and a symbolic link with the great temple at Avebury.

Other Stones

Leslie Grinsell also mentions "two stones just west of a cow-house" at Middle Ham, Tynings, on the western side of the village. I would agree that their position, towards Chew Magna, probably excludes them from any visual alignment: "These have been considered by some to have formed that part of the Stanton Drew group, but this is very doubtful."

Kelly's Directory, for 1889, mentions "an isolated fragment" near Sandy Lane.

Continuation from page 24:
John Aubrey's description
of Stanton Drew in
the 1660s

The Cove

Dominating the beer-garden between the Druids' Arms and the parish church are two immense standing stones, 10 feet apart and of similar height, one being a 12-foot monster, with a great flat boulder lying between them (ST 598 631).

Leslie Grinsell points out that the distance and space between them would have been sufficient for them to have formed a Neolithic chambered long barrow. In fact the fallen stone is of the right size to have functioned as a capstone. Not that Leslie Grinsell was convinced.

Coves may also exist in their own right, standing inside "the northern inner circle at Avebury, the earliest phase of Cairnapple Hill in Midlothian, and possibly the 'Whispering Knights' at Rollright in Oxfordshire". As Grinsell goes on to say, there are also precedents such as the recumbent stone between two uprights which are a characteristic feature of the so-called Recumbent Stone Circles of Aberdeenshire, which "may have had the same function as 'coves', but no plausible suggestion as to the nature of that function has yet been made".

Coves, the cynic might add, are any setting of stones which archaeologists stumble across as they make their way from the nearest public house. That is literally the case at Stanton Drew.

The Druids' Arms

Having the Cove in its grounds, the Druids' Arms Inn (I've positioned the apostrophe on the assumption that is was named for more than one Druid) cements in the modern mind whatever link the Druids and pre-Celtic Stanton Drew arguably lacked in reality, with the association dating from comparatively recent times (ST 597 632). It was an inspired name change, which evolved from the Foresters' Arms of John Coward and William Sherborne Perry's time, through the second half of Queen Victoria's reign and into the Edwardian decade.

William Stukeley would certainly have endorsed the change:

> I make no doubt but the name of Stanton Drue is derived from our Monument; Stanton from the stones, and Drue from the Druids. It moves me not, that some of the name of Drew might have lived here formely; for such a family might take the denomination of the town, and, leaving out the first part, retain only that of Drew. It is sufficient conviction, that there are so many other towns in England, and elsewhere, that have preserved this name, and all remarkable for monuments of nature.

For good measure, the village can also offer Druid View, and Druids' Peep. John Newcombe is the landlord at the Druids' Arms. He also keeps the mediaeval legend alive: "The explanation is that the circles are of dancing guests at a wedding party who were turned to stone. Those in my back garden are the bride, the bridegroom, and the best man."

He didn't say which of the three had fallen down on the job.

Circular Walk

Somerset's premier ancient monument is now in the care of English Heritage and can be visited on the course of this six mile walk, now described, which I compiled for Somerset Magazine. The circuit initially heads out of the village, beside the Cove and the Druids' Arms. Our route then heads east to pass between slag-heaps of the former Somerset coal-field, and into the historic former main street of Pensford, complete with Georgian lock-up.

We then cross the River Chew – noting its flood marker at the top of a downstairs window – and follow it under the great series of arches which carried a branch line of the Great Western Railway southwards from Bristol to Radstock and Frome. This viaduct is the other great monument of the walk, after which we cross a pastoral landscape that returns us to the stones.

Conditions under foot are liable to be wet in places, with some of the damp patches persisting for much of the year. Apart from that, and a few arable fields, the paths are otherwise reasonably well marked and negotiable with a number of newish stiles and signs.

Park and start from Stanton Drew, which is south of the dinky pixie-like thatched turnpike Toll House on the B3130 east of Chew Magna, and set off southwards from the Druid's Arms (Ordnance Survey map reference ST 597 632).

To the left, in the corner of the beer garden, is the Cove setting of three huge stones.

Continue straight ahead at the junction with Upper Stanton, up Bromley Road. Note the exposed red sandstone stratum, beyond the next house on the right.

Box Bush follows, then bungalows and Auden House and the Drive.

Turn left between the Crescent and the next junction, eastwards across a stile opposite No.7. Follow the hedgerow straight ahead and skirt the left side of Twinway Farm.

A second public path then turns right, southwards, following the farm drive to the east end of the Dutch barn. Then follow the dirt track into the fields and bear right, to keep the hedgerow on our right as we head south.

Go through the gate near the corner of the field, to follow it for the final few yards to the road opposite the entrance to Curls Farm.

Turn left, along the road, south-east to Bromley Farm. Here we turn left and then right, into the farmyard. Cross it diagonally, to the left of the stone outbuilding on triple arches.

Turn right in the field, north-eastwards, keeping the hedge to your right, and then cross the stile beside the ditch in 100 yards. There are three paths from here and ours is straight ahead, continuing north-east, down to the left-hand side of the tree-clad slag heap. The coal mine was further across to the right.

Here again there are two paths and ours is straight ahead. In 150 yards we turn left, across a footbridge over a ditch, and then turn right in the field.

Follow the dense hedgerow. In 100 yards we turn right, across a stream and stile. Proceed straight ahead in the next field, heading eastwards and upwards, with the stream to your right.

Cross the stile in the corner and continue straight

ahead, up the slope to a stile in the hedge on the other side. Then follow the next hedge straight ahead, up the hill, heading south-east.

We pass over the course of a dismantled tramway, running from the colliery to the railway, though it is almost invisible.

Towards the top of the hill we keep well to the right of Stanton Wick, via a stile in the fence below the power line. In the next field we then bear left, towards the closest cottage and into Stanton Wick.

Exit from the field between the houses and the bungalows. There is a stile to the right of the gate.

Turn left at the road and follow it around to the right at Keppelgate, with its unusual shaped cottage that has a curving back wall. We are heading north-east.

Pass the Carpenters' Arms and go over the hill at Parsons Farm.

At the corner we turn right, across a stile in the hedge 20 yards before the field gate. Turn left on the other side and keep the hedge to your left, as we continue north-eastwards.

Proceed straight ahead, beside the cattle trough, into the next field. Our second disused colliery is in woodland below and to the left.

Cross into the undergrowth at the bottom corner of the field. Proceed straight ahead, through the holly bushes, and cross Salter's Brook.

On the other side we turn left through the brambles and then right, up the slope. On the summit we continue straight ahead across the overgrown track-bed of a disused railway.

Beyond it we follow the conifer hedge and wall to

emerge on the A37 beside Pensford House at Whitley Batts.

Cross it into Birchwood Lane. In the dip in 200 yards we turn left across the stile, immediately before the drive to Sandhills.

Follow the hedgerow straight ahead, northwards to a farm track. This takes us over the hill.

Skirt to the left of the final field before Pensford. Turn right at the road, down into the village, along Pensford Old Road, which used to be the main road.

Lower down, in the High Street, we pass the former miners' cottages, with a pebbled raised pavement beside the Old Bakery. Next is Green's Folly, dated 1782, followed by the imposing George and Dragon. The beehived-shaped Georgian lock-up is on the right at the junction.

From here we turn left, down to the modern main road, and head for the parish church. History now abounds. Spot the "Flood Level" of 10th July 1968, opposite the war memorial, eight feet up at the top of the downstairs window. Uncomfortable; having to sleep on that.

Then we approach the offending River Chew. Eighteenth-century Bridge House, to the left, has Salter's Brook beneath it.

Turn left beside Bridge House and then immediately right, to pass Sally Higgins Cottage.

Turn right opposite the farm, through a kissing gate, to go under the riverside arch of Pensford Viaduct. Don't look up.

Now follow the River Chew, keeping it to your right. In the following field we continue straight ahead, as the river bends to the right.

Then in the next field we are closer to the river on the approach to Byemills Farm. Pass to the left of it and then proceed straight ahead, across the stile into the field facing us.

Keep the river to your right. We are heading south-west, to Upper Stanton Drew. Cross stiles in the next field, about 50 yards to the left of the river.

We then cross higher ground, beside an ash tree, to follow the power cables. Then a hedge brings us to a road, to the right of a Gothic-arched packhorse bridge, below Brook Cottage.

Cross into the arable field on the south side of the road and follow its right-hand hedgerow.

Also cross the next road in 250 yards, westwards into the fruit field on the other side. We are now heading for the tower of St Mary's church, back in Stanton Drew.

At the end of the field we cross a stile in the dense hedgerow, 40 yards to the left of the power line. Beyond it we resume heading westwards, again aiming for the church tower.

Cross the stile beside the gate and walk up the slope. Join the farm road in the top right-hand corner of the field and then cross the stiles beside its gates.

At the next corner we glance right, for a view of the Great Circle and the North Eastern Circle beyond it, with a short avenue of big stones linking the two. The South Western Circle is up on the rise to the left, with a view across to the church and over the valley.

To visit the stones we turn right at the farm and walk down to Court Farm House. Then turn right via the honesty box to cross the pasture to the Great Circle and the outlying stones behind it. On turning around, to complete the megalithic experience, we now cross the field, diagonally, and head for the South Western Circle. The access path (which is a pay path rather than a public one, covered by the money in the box) takes us across our original route in the next field and then over another boundary to the stones in the corner of the following field.

From here we return to the farm road and then back into the village, via the church and its exceedingly ancient font, to the main street and the Druids' Arms. Druids worshipped in sylvan groves, as well as among ancient stones, but their Celtic wisdom is the thread of religious continuity between the pagan temple and the Christian church.

WALK MAP

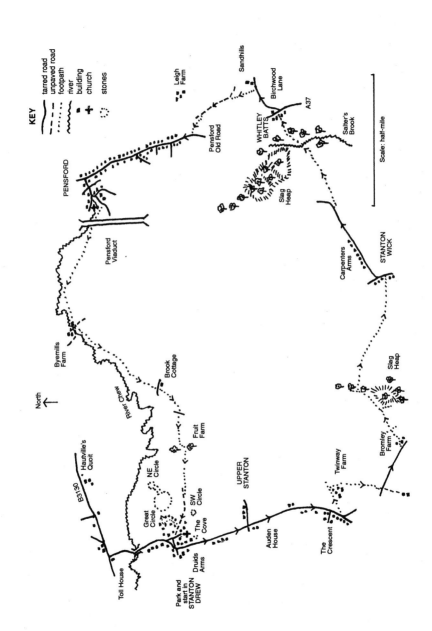

KEY
- tarred road
- unpaved road
- footpath
- river
- building
- church
- stones

North ←

Scale: half-mile

Hautville's Quoit

B3130

Toll House

Byemills Farm

PENSFORD

Pensford Viaduct

Pensford Old Road

Leigh Farm

Sandhills

Birchwood Lane

A37

WHITLEY BATTS

Salter's Brook

Slag Heap

River Chew

Brook Cottage

Great Circle

NE Circle

SW Circle

The Cove

Fruit Farm

Druids Arms

Park and start in STANTON DREW

UPPER STANTON

Auden House

The Crescent

Twinway Farm

Bromley Farm

Slag Heap

Carpenters Arms

STANTON WICK

Bibliography

1664 John Aubrey. *Monumenta Britannica.* First published nearly three centuries later, by Dorset Publishing Company, Milborne Port, 1980-82. Two volumes, edited by John Fowles, with annotations by Rodney Legg.

1660s Robert Gay. *A Fool's Bolt soon shott at Stonage.* First published decades later, by T. Hearne in *Peter Langtoft's Chronicle,* London, 1725. See Volume Two. Printed in *Stonehenge Antiquaries* by Rodney Legg, 1986, which is distributed by Halsgrove, Tiverton.

1776 William Stukeley. *Itinerarium Curiosum.* Two volumes, recording his fieldwork of 1723. See Volume Two.

1792 Rev John Collinson. *The History of Antiquaries of the County of Somerset.* Three volumes, published in Bath. See Volume Two.

1821 Rev S. Seyer. *History of Bristol.* See Volume One.

1826 Sir Richard Colt Hoare. *Modern Wiltshire.* See Volume Two.

1850s J. Whereat, publisher. *The Petrified Wedding: or a Tale of the Druidical Remains at Stanton Drew.*

1858 W. Long. Report on Stanton Drew in *The Archaeological Journal,* Volume 15.

1869 George W. Nelson and W. Way. *The Fairy Ring: a Legend of Stanton Drew, or the Wicked Wedding Party who were turned into Stone for Dancing on Sunday.* Playlet of a performance at the Theatre Royal, Bath, in April 1869.

1880 C. P. Kains-Jackson. *Our Ancient Monuments and the Land Around Them.* Contains an account of the legend, rendered with poetic licence.

1887 E. Boger. *Myths, Stones, and Worthies of Somerset.* Also concentrates on repeating the folklore.

1887 Professor C. Lloyd Morgan. Report on "The Stones of Stanton Drew, their Source and Origin" in the *Proceedings of the Somerset Archaeological Society,* Volume 33.

1889 *Kelly's Directory of Somersetshire.* Relays James Fergusson's dotty Arthurian dating.

1896 C. W. Dymond. *Stanton Drew,* a booklet which ran to several editions, with the 40-page large paper edition, limited to 162 copies, being the fullest version.

1909 Sir William Watson. Poem on Stanton Drew, first published in *The Spectator,* London, September 1909.

1913 E. Sibree. *Stanton Drew.* Pamphlet published in Bristol.

1922 R. R. C. Gregory. *Poems in Dialect,* being Volume 5 in the Somerset Folk Series. Its contribution is "Thik Weddin' at Stanton Drew".

1924 D. M. Cary. *Some Ballad Legends of Somerset,* which is Volume 14 of the Somerset Folk Series. Reprints a poem on Stanton Drew by Miss M. Coates and her sister.

1956 L. V. Grinsell. *Stanton Drew Stone Circles, Somerset.* Ministry of Works guide to the monument, published by Her Majesty's Stationery Office.

1973 L. V. Grinsell. *The Folklore of Stanton Drew.* Booklet, published in Guernsey by the Toucan Press.

1997 Nigel Hawkes. "Woodhenge find rivals stone circles," being a page feature in *The Times,* London, for 11 November 1997. This was the most detailed of numerous accounts to appear that day in national and regional newspapers, as well as on television and radio.

1998 Rodney Legg. "Walk: Stanton Drew and Pensford," in *Somerset Magazine,* March 1998.

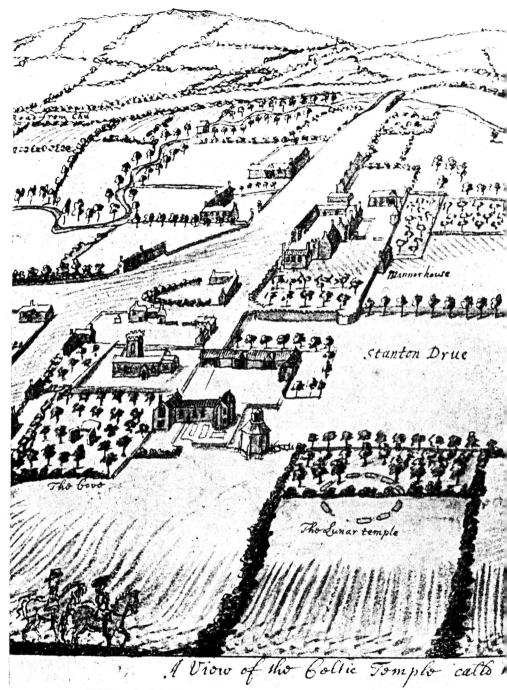

Read from Chu

Manner house

Stanton Drue

The Cove

The Lunar temple

A View of the Celtic Temple called

William Stukeley's drawing: 'A View of the Celtic Temple called the Weddings at Stanton Drew, July 1723'

Chue river

Road to Pennisford

Hauteuils cot

The planetary Temple

The Solar Temple

The fidlers

oddings at Stanton Drue July 1723.

William Stukeley's print: A View of Stanton Drew, 23 July 1723.
Published 1776

Misknol

William Stukeley's print: A View at Stanton Drew. 1776

William Stukeley's print: The Cove at Stanton Drew. 1776

*Hautville's Quoit: John Aubrey's
revised version of his text on
'Hakewell's Coyte' from
Monumenta Britannica*

About a quarter of a mile from this monument of
the *Wedding*, is another great stone called
Hakewell's Coyte, which may be ... the ...
remains of the like Monument. In these
parts lived anciently one *Hakewell* a person
of great estate, and great strength of Body,
he lies interred in (New-church where he
hath a Monument.

    Drew is the name of an ancient Family
in the Westerne parts: so I will not ...
to straine the etymologie of this place too
much, to my owne Hypothesis: but leave it
at a Quære.

which is a great country stone, of the shape of a coyte, and lies
flatt, and seemes to have been [...]: it is of the same sort of
stone with those at the *Wedding*. this is not erect as those
of *Stoneheng &c.* the common-people tell the incredible story
that *Hakewell* stood upon the top of Norton-hill, about
half a mile off where the Coyte now lies, and coyted it downe
to this place: for which having the Mannor of Norton given
him, and thinking it too little, He gives it the name of Norton-
Mal-rewarde, which they pronounce Smalreward.

    That in these parts anciently was one *Hakewell* a
person of great estate and strength of Body is manifest by
figure in his monument in (New-church.

    from &c. this Information is from my worthy friend Mr [...].

[Handwritten manuscript text by John Aubrey, largely illegible cursive. Legible fragments include: "...break them with sledges, because they so crumble..." "...and they told me, [1664] they are much diminished within these few years." "...This Monument is much bigger than Stonehenge. the Diameter is ninety paces. I could not perceive any Trench about it as at Stonehenge &c: it is in ploughed land, and consequently easily worn-out. When I last saw this, it was in Harvest-time, and the Barley being then ripe, I could not come to survey the Stones so exactly as I would otherwise have done: but this Scheme (as it is) resembleth it." "The Stones a a a a &c seeme to be the remainder of the Avenue, as at Kynet, and Aubury; the length of the Avenue is about halfe a quarter of a mile: and the stones d d d might be a leading to another Temple; as from West-Kynet to the Temple on the top of the Hill: is the Scheme." "I doe presume, that the like Approaches (or Avenues) were at Stonehenge, and at Rollrich, as are here, though now decayed by time. — Northeastward from Stonehenge is a stone a good distance off, which seames (to me) to be the remaine of it: and the stone called the Kings-stone at Rollrich seames to be so too. see the Schemes of both Temples;"]

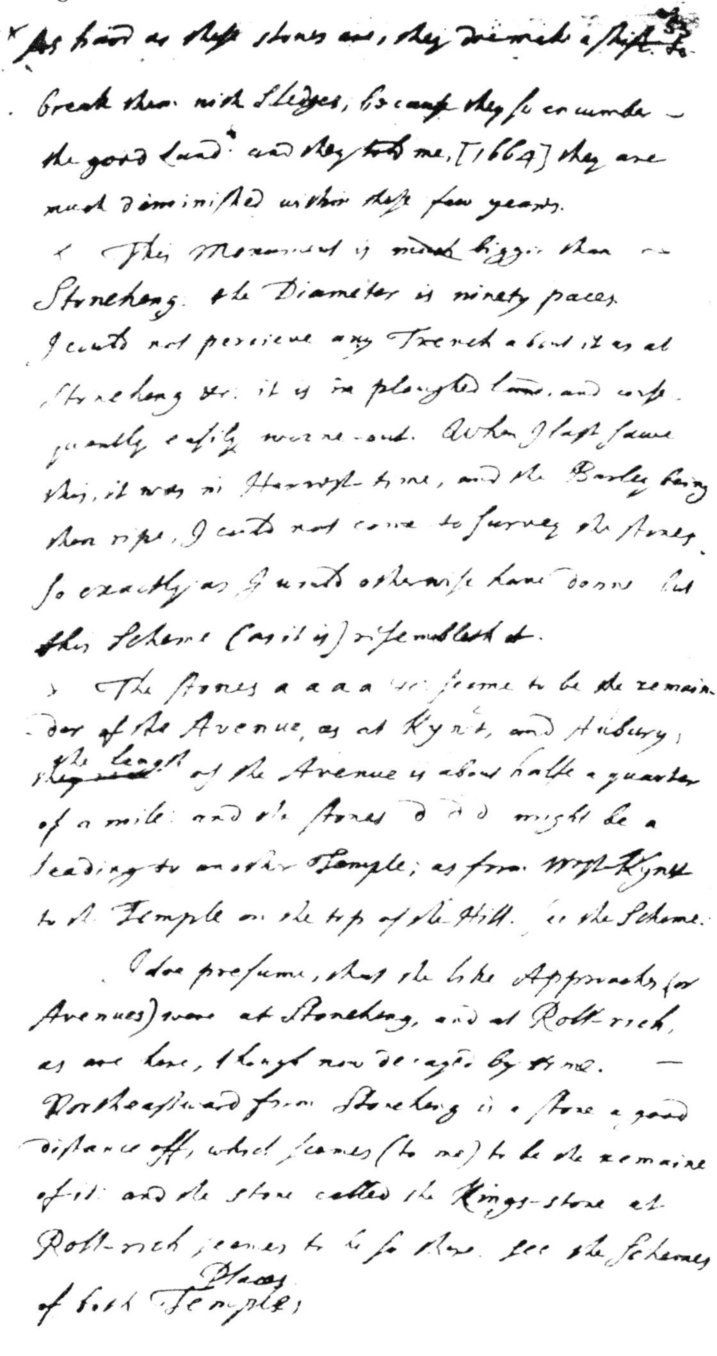

51

Index